FREEZER BURN

Oxymorons and Other Contradictions
of Everyday Life

Laine Vilensky
David Holmes
Jeff MacNelly

Ballantine Books • New York

Library of Congress Catalog Card Number: 90-93259

ISBN: 0-345-36570-4

Manufactured in the United States of America

Cover illustration by Jeff MacNelly

First Edition: March 1991
10 9 8 7 6 5 4 3 2 1

Civil War

Perfect Idiot

Original Copy

Mandatory Option

Working Vacation

Foxy Chick

Evaporated Milk

Fresh Frozen

Elementary Calculus

Omnibus
Cookie
Protection
Act

Cookies

Congressional Ethics

Divorce Court

Partially Completed

Live Television

Rap Music.

Unacceptable Solution

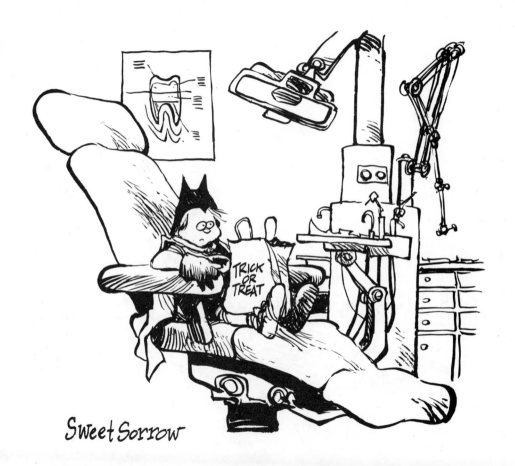

Sweet Sorrow

Minor Disaster

Non-Stop Flight

Plastic Glasses

Dodge Ram

Cherokee Pioneer

Mobil Station

Flexible Freeze

Airline Food

Dry Wine

Peacekeeper Missile

Black Light

Great Depression

Baby Grand

Old News

Industrial Park

Work Party

Standard Deviation

Criminal Justice

Down Escalator

Death Benefits

Student Teacher

Pretty Ugly

Irate Patient

Freezer Burn

Alone Together

Advanced Basic

Athletic Scholarship

Educational Television

Sensible Shoes

Terribly Nice

Republican Party

Sure Bet

Junk Food

Random Logic

Light Heavyweight

Holy War

Guest Host

Gourmet Pizza

Nuclear Safety

Marijuana Initiative

Jumbo Shrimp

Fast Idle

Passive Aggression

Marital Bliss